Fiction 5

Series Editor: Pie Corbett

CAMBRIDGE
UNIVERSITY PRESS

CAMBRIDGE UNIVERSITY PRESS
Cambridge, New York, Melbourne, Madrid, Cape Town, Singapore, São Paulo

Cambridge University Press
The Edinburgh Building, Cambridge CB2 2RU, UK

www.cambridge.org
Information on this title: www.cambridge.org/9780521618892

First published 2006

Printed in the United Kingdom at the University Press, Cambridge

A catalogue record for this publication is available from the British Library

ISBN-13   978-0-521-61889-2 paperback
ISBN-10   0-521-61889-4 paperback

ACKNOWLEDGEMENTS

Cover
Beehive Illustration (Pulsar)

Artwork

Beehive Illustration (Russell Becker, Pulsar)

Texts

Significant author: 'The Shadow Thief' by Margaret Mahy
Traditional tales: 'The Laidley Worm' retold by Chris Buckton
Stories from a variety of cultures: 'A Long Way Home' by Pratima Mitchell

Contents

Significant author

The Shadow Thief

Chapter One

"Oliver," said Mrs McMarvel to her dear, and only, son. "I've found just the right house for us. We're shifting in next Friday."

"Is it cheap?" asked Oliver. He knew that, given half a chance, his mother would always spend too much money. He had to watch over her.

"Very cheap," she said, but she was looking a bit unreliable as she said it. "And it's right on the edge of town."

"Good," said Oliver. "That means you'll be able to practise your bagpipes without upsetting anyone. Anyone except me, that is!"

His mother loved to play the bagpipes, but she played them very badly. Neighbours complained and sometimes called the police, saying that Mrs McMarvel was creating a nuisance.

"It has a sunny back garden so there will be roll-around room for Morris-the-Cat," Mrs McMarvel continued. Morris-the-Cat heard this and began to purr. "And it doesn't leak much. Mind you, there is one teeny-tiny thing I ought to mention…"

"What?" Oliver cried, full of sudden suspicion. Morris-the-Cat stopped purring.

"Well," said Mrs McMarvel. "There's one house next door, over the fence. And it's a haunted house. That's why our house is so cheap."

Oliver relaxed, and Morris-the-Cat started purring again.

"Haunted, eh?" said Oliver. "It's lucky that we're both so brave, isn't it?"

They moved in on Friday … bulging suitcases, great flopping mattresses, and many cartons cracking at the corners but held together with strong hairy string. Oliver had a bedroom big enough to swing a cat in, which was probably why Morris-the-Cat immediately shot out into the garden. Oliver made his bed, shelved his books in his bookcase, and wound up his frog-clock, carefully placing it on the top shelf. He hung his lion-kite on the wall, set his running shoes side by side under his bed, and tied his crocodile-mask to the back of the door, arranging it so that it could look across the room and watch him reading in bed. *Everything's perfect*, thought Oliver, jubilantly.

But then his mother began her bagpipe practice. She marched from room to room playing so badly that Oliver fell flat on the floor and rolled around with his fingers in his ears. The house was not quite perfect, after all.

And, to make matters worse, that very first night in his very new bedroom, Oliver woke up to find that he was being haunted.

Chapter Two

His frog-clock croaked midnight ... twelve long, loud croaks. Oliver's sheets – both the one under him and the one over him – grew suddenly cold and then even colder. His teeth began to chatter so loudly that the chattering woke him up. It felt as if someone was tap-dancing deep inside his head.

He was not alone. Oliver knew that immediately. He propped himself up on his freezing elbows and peered into the night. Yes! There, at the end of his bed, he made out a figure both black and silvery in the midnight gloom. A swirling mist of long hair rose and fell around it. And the face in the middle of that hair was like a sort of everlasting firework – exploding, but exploding silently, putting itself together once more, staring around at the world and then exploding all over again.

"Who are you?" Oliver asked, as well as he could between his tap-dancing teeth.

"I am a ghost," said the ghost. "I am sick of haunting my own house next door. There's never anyone there to terrify, so I have come to terrify you."

"You won't t-t-t-terrify me," chattered Oliver. "I'm not t-t-t-terrifyable."

But this was not quite true. As he watched the ghost-face explode silently yet again, as its wild hair rose in the air, looping and fraying out like strings of smoke, Oliver wanted to duck down between his cold sheets, shut his eyes and lie there screaming until the ghost had gone. On the other hand, he didn't want to give the ghost any satisfaction.

"I can hear your teeth chattering," said the ghost.

"They're only t-t-t-tap-dancing," said Oliver. "I'm very musical. Even my teeth are musical." The sheets were icy by now. His pillow, in its clean pillowcase, felt like a drift of snow. "My mother is musical too. She plays the b-b-b-bagpipes."

"OK!" said the ghost. "I'm going to haunt you. Watch me haunting." It drifted up into the air, looped the loop, swung on the light, then twisted around it like a shining serpent.

"Pretty good, eh?" it cried, full of admiration for itself.

"Anyone could d-d-d-do that," said Oliver. "I w-would, only I can't b-b-b-be b-b-b-bothered getting out of b-b-b-bed." But this was not quite true either. (I am terrified, Oliver was thinking incredulously. So this is what terror feels like!)

Then the ghost put out a long, thin, silvery hand and peeled the shadow of Oliver's lion-kite from the wall. It drifted towards the closed door and somehow dissolved through the solid wood, taking the kite-shadow along with it.

Oliver's sheets immediately began to warm up, and (after a bit of tossing and turning) he managed to sleep until the morning sun chased the moon from the sky and grinned brightly in at his window.

"You're looking very thoughtful," said his mother at breakfast time. "Is everything all right? Did you sleep well?"

"I was just thinking about flying my lion-kite," said Oliver. "There's plenty of space in this garden and there's a good breeze today."

There was a good breeze. It bustled around the corner of the house and leaped out at Oliver and his kite. But no matter how high Oliver held that kite, no matter how he tugged it and ran with it, it refused to fly. Oliver stood looking down at it, slumped and sad on the lawn. Then he looked around carefully. The trees had pillowy shadows, the hollyhocks had long

leaning shadows, the fence between his house and the house next door cast a shadow, too. But the lion-kite had no shadow and without a shadow it was a dead kite.

"Who'd have thought that a shadow would make such a difference," said Oliver, looking at his own shadow with new interest. But right then, his mother started her bagpipe practice, playing much worse than usual, and Oliver forgot his shadowless kite. He had something else to worry about.

That night, Oliver's frog-clock croaked twelve times and Oliver woke up, shaking and shivering between sheets of ice. There was the ghost, still exploding, still drifting. Oliver's teeth began their tap-dancing.

"Did you try to fly your kite?" the ghost asked him, mockingly. "Didn't fly, did it? I'll bet you're frightened of me now."

"I'm shivering because of the c-c-cold," said Oliver.

"I'm stealing more shadows tonight," said the ghost. "You'll soon be terrified of me!" And it dissolved through the door, its face silently exploding as it looked back over its shoulder. Oliver's bed began to warm up once more and he slid back into sleep.

Chapter Three

The sun chased the moon out of the sky. Oliver woke up, dressed, and went to put on his running shoes. But for some reason, they felt clammy on his bare feet. The laces draped themselves across his fingers like cold spaghetti. When he tried to walk, he slipped and stumbled, and, slipping and stumbling, he noticed that his shadow legs ended just below the ankles. No feet!

Oliver knew at once what this meant. The shadows of his running shoes had been stolen away. He had slipped his feet into dead running shoes. But worse was to come.

"Stop flopping around," said Mrs McMarvel, as he stumbled up behind her, but she wasn't really looking at Oliver. She was too worried about Morris-the-Cat. "Morris isn't very well," she said. "He won't wake up properly."

"He probably needs a break from your bagpipe practice," said Oliver, staring across his mother's shoulder at Morris-the-Cat, who lay on the sofa as limp as a toy cat that had lost half its stuffing. Apart from his green eyes, which occasionally blinked, Morris-the-Cat was like a dead cat. And then Oliver saw that Morris-the-Cat – Morris-the-lively-leaping-about-cat – had lost his shadow.

Fear rose up in Oliver, but almost immediately fury chased it away.

"OK!" he muttered. "Right! Two can play at that game." He began to plan his campaign. He was terrified, of course, but he wasn't going to let mere terror bother him. Oliver had made up his mind to haunt the ghost.

Oliver plotted and planned until he heard his frog-clock croaking twelve. Midday! Lunch wasn't ready yet. Mrs McMarvel was far too busy fussing over Morris-the-Cat to cook anything, but Oliver didn't care. It is easier to haunt when you feel like a skeleton. He tiptoed upstairs, unhooked his crocodile-mask and then stole his mother's bagpipes from beside her bed. With the bagpipes tucked under his left arm and his crocodile-mask dangling from his right hand, he shot across the lawn and scrambled over the fence, making for the back door of the haunted house.

The back door was locked, but when Oliver rattled a window, the window catch came out of the rotting sill, making a horrid squelching sound as it did so, and the window swung open. Of course Oliver was utterly terrified but he was getting used to terror by now. Up he went and in he went. The window flopped shut behind him.

Though the summer sun was hot on the grass outside, the haunted house was utterly dark and damp and shadowy. Oliver hooked his crocodile-mask over his ears and began haunting.

"Oooooo!" he howled in a crocodile-voice. "I'm here! I'm haunting you."

Every empty room in the haunted house howled back at him. "OOooooooo!"

It was quite a chorus.

"Ghost! Ghost! I know you're there," yelled Oliver. "I'm coming to get you." He pulled the string that snapped the crocodile's jaws. Snapping and shouting in his most eerie voice, he prowled from room to room. Nothing! Nothing and no one!

"Come out you coward!" he cried. "I'm looking for you." He opened cupboards and smelt mildew. Hundreds of spiders scuttled ahead of him into damp cracks and crannies in the rotting floor. He climbed the stairs and they twitched uneasily under his feet; he searched right, then left, and came, finally, into the last room of all. And there, for the first time in that rotting, sunless house, he saw shadows – the shadow of a kite on the wall, the shadow of running shoes on the floor and the shadow of a cat stretched out beside them.

"OOooooo!" howled Oliver. "I am the haunting McMarvel, and I'm haunting YOU."

Chapter Four

Something stirred. Something whispered.

"Go away!" said the whispering something. "I sleep during the daytime. And anyhow it's my job to haunt you, and it's your job to be terrified. That's a law of nature."

"So you want to sleep," wailed Oliver. "Then I'll play you a lullaby!"

Hooking the bagpipes under his arm, he began to play. Oliver's mother played the bagpipes badly, but Oliver was even worse.

The ghost leaped up, exploding desperately.

"Stop it! Stop it! I need sleep or I'll begin to fade."

"This is the McMarvel bagpipe sonata," explained Oliver. "And now you have interrupted me, I'll have to begin again." And he did. The whole house shook hideously to the sound of badly played bagpipes.

"Stop it! Please!" said the ghost, and now it was begging. "Those bagpipe vibrations are tearing me to bits. Look! I'm starting to show up in the daylight, and that's fatal for ghosts."

Indeed it was becoming easier and easier to see the ghost. Oliver could look deep into its hollow eyes. "You're terrifying me," it cried.

"Then bring those shadows back," commanded Oliver. "Promise to bring them back tonight or I'll be here bagpiping tomorrow. My kite won't fly without its shadow. My running shoes won't run. And Morris-the-Cat just lies around, all limp and languid. We need our shadows more than you do."

And just to emphasise his words, he played the first bars of the McMarvel bagpipe sonata for the third time.

"OK!" screamed the ghost. "OK! OK! I will. I will. I only stole them to make a bit of fun for myself. It gets very boring being a ghost and haunting an empty house."

"Boring?" said Oliver. "I didn't know ghosts could get bored." He looked around the haunted house. He studied its bare walls and its rotting sills. He looked down at the dusty floor.

"I spend all night wandering and wailing," the ghost went on. "But there's no one to hear me. I was so thrilled when you moved in next door. Someone to terrify, I thought. But then it turned out to be you. I'm the unluckiest ghost there ever was."

"Hang on," said Oliver. "Let's talk it over. Maybe we can work something out. I mean you'll have to give Morris-the-Cat his shadow again, but I'll lend you the shadow of the kite for a few nights. You can fly it by moonlight. And what if you came over tonight and stole the bagpipe-shadow? Would shadow *vibrations* bother you? Because I think any ghost playing the bagpipes would be more terrifying than most ghosts. Particularly if it played them badly."

The ghost's face exploded with sudden hope.

"I don't know," it said. "I just don't know, but it's worth a go."

"And we could haunt each other," Oliver went on. "That might be fun. We'll give it that go you mentioned, and then we'll know."

Ooooooo

Chapter Five

The next morning (after the sun had chased the moon from the sky) as Oliver made his way downstairs, something leaped out at him. It was Morris-the-Cat, playful as ever, with his shadow leaping beside him. Mrs McMarvel sat at the table, her bagpipes lying at her feet. Oliver could see at once that, even in the sunlit kitchen, they were casting no shadow at all.

"Good morning," Mrs McMarvel said. "It's bright and breezy. Are you going to fly your kite today?"

"Maybe tomorrow," said Oliver. "Are you going to play your bagpipes?"

"I was going to," said his mother, "but, somehow or other, I can't get a squeak out of them. They've gone all floppy, and who wants floppy bagpipes? I don't think I'll play them any more."

Oliver tried to look sympathetic, but he couldn't help grinning with relief. *I'll say thank you to the ghost when I go over to haunt him later today,* he thought.

"I'll give up the bagpipes," his mother said, "but a musical person has to play something. I think I'll take violin lessons. Mind you, I'll have to practise. I'll be at it morning, noon and night."

And, thinking of his mother learning to play the violin, and having to practise morning, noon and night, Oliver was really terrified.

The Laidley Worm

Chapter One

The New Queen

Long ago, in distant times, Northumbria was ruled by a good and kind king. He had a gentle, loving wife, and one daughter, Margaret, who was as beautiful as a May morning. But alas, the King's beloved wife died, and he was overcome with grief.

Now, although the King was good and kind, he was not always wise. In his grief, he sailed away from Bamburgh Castle, leaving his daughter alone and unhappy.

Margaret longed for her father to return. Each day, she stood on the castle wall and looked out to sea. Each day, she held the castle keys in her hand and made a wish to bring him safely back. Each day, she threw the keys over her left shoulder to bring him luck.

But each day she was disappointed.

Meanwhile, time passed, and Margaret's father began to forget his dead wife. The good and kind but rather foolish King had been enchanted by a raven-haired lady from the wild Land-in-the-West. She was not all she seemed, for underneath her beauty there was an evil soul. But the King did not see into her true heart. He fell in love with the raven-haired lady and made her his wife. He set sail for Castle Bamburgh, and with him came all the lords of the North Country for a great feast in her honour.

And so it was that, at last, Margaret's patience was rewarded. One morning, as she gazed out to sea, she saw sails glinting in the sun. A great fleet of ships was approaching. The castle servants rang the bells to welcome their king with his new queen.

Margaret was full of joy to see her father again. She ran to meet him at the castle gate.

"My beloved daughter!" cried the King, hugging her close to him. "You have grown into a most beautiful woman since I have been away. How I have missed you! But see now, I have brought you a new mother. It is my dearest wish that you and she will be happy together."

"Welcome, dear Father, welcome back to your castle! And welcome too, dear Stepmother. The castle is yours to enjoy." And Margaret handed the new Queen the keys of the castle. The fingers that grasped the keys were hard and cold, but the voice was full of smiles and kisses.

"Sweet girl," she crooned. "We shall be the best of friends."

Chapter Two

The Feast

At the wedding feast, Margaret's beauty and grace amazed the guests. One of the lords spoke out loudly to all at the table and raised his glass. "Let us drink to the Lady Margaret! This princess is the fairest creature I have ever seen!"

The new Queen looked sharply at the lord. "I think you have forgotten your Queen!" She laughed lightly but her thoughts were bitter. She did not like the attention Margaret was getting. Why should this girl steal everyone's love? Even the King looked at Margaret more often than at her. Jealousy boiled in her wicked heart. "I shall use my witchcraft to teach her a lesson," she thought. "I shall bring her low. If she wasn't here, all this love would be mine."

Margaret did not know of her stepmother's jealousy. She was happy to have her father home again, and she was deceived by the Queen's pretended kindness. The castle was no longer sad and gloomy. Lights shone brightly and huge fires blazed in the hearths. Music and laughter filled the halls, and wonderful embroidered tapestries were hung in the bedrooms.

The next day, when the family dined in the great hall, the Queen was bedecked with sumptuous jewels. Emeralds sparkled on her white throat, diamonds glittered in her raven hair, and rings of ruby decorated her long fingers. Margaret was dazzled by her stepmother. She could see too that her father was happy again.

The Queen smiled fondly and stroked Margaret's cheek. "Dear girl," she purred, "I must find a jewel for you. Come to my chamber after supper, and you may choose what you will from my treasure chest."

Margaret suspected nothing. After dinner, she followed her stepmother to her private chamber. A servant saw her laughing happily in the doorway.

That was the last time she was seen.

The next morning, when servants reported that Margaret was missing, the King was troubled. Where could his beloved daughter be?

"What happened after dinner?" he asked his wife. "Did she choose a jewel?"

The Queen smiled sadly. "Oh yes." Her voice was soft. "She took a necklace of pearls. She said she would walk awhile on the shore to see the sunset. Perhaps she…"

"Perhaps?"

"Who knows what dangers lurk there…" The Queen sounded full of fear.

The King sprang up in alarm. "We must send men to search along the sea."

Chapter Three

The Strange Beast

For seven days and seven nights the King's servants searched the lonely coast. They hunted for Margaret among the gloomy caves and rocks that surrounded the castle.

There was no sign of her.

Then on the eighth day, a messenger brought terrible news. The men had found the lair of a strange beast, high up on the cliffs. They had found bones outside its cave. They had seen the terrible creature, a huge snake, with fiery breath that burned the grass and set fire to the trees.

"It is the fearsome Laidley Worm of Spindleston," gasped the Queen. "I have heard stories of this snake. It has killed your beloved daughter. It will lay waste to our land." She turned her head to hide her smile. She hoped that the King's fear for his people would make him forget Margaret.

But the King was overcome with grief. He could not stir from his bed to save his people. He could think of nothing but his daughter's terrible death.

Meanwhile, the Laidley Worm roamed around the countryside. It blasted the fields with its fiery breath. It laid waste to the farmers' crops with its poison that was so venomous no blade of grass could grow within seven miles of the castle. It devoured sheep and cattle, and children too, if unwary parents let them stray. At night it wrapped its scaly folds round Spindleston Hill.

The people were desperate. To try and stop it from killing the sheep, they brought it fresh milk from seven cows. Every morning and every night they filled a stone trough outside the monster's cave. Every morning and every night the worm greedily gulped up the milk, slobbering and slurping. But it was all in vain. The worm still uncoiled its loathsome scaly folds each morning to writhe and wriggle across the countryside, killing everything in its path.

The people came to the castle and begged to speak to their king. "The Laidley Worm has killed all our livestock.

Now it is killing our children," said one bold farmer. "Sire, you know what it is to lose a beloved daughter. For her sake, we beseech you to help us."

At last the King roused himself. "We must send word," he said. "We must send word east and west and over the sea. We must spread the news far and wide that the Laidley Worm is ruining the North Country."

Chapter Four

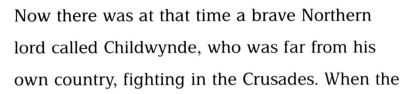

Childwynde to the Rescue

Now there was at that time a brave Northern lord called Childwynde, who was far from his own country, fighting in the Crusades. When the tale of the dreaded Laidley Worm reached him, he was filled with woe. "Alas, that my land and all its people should live in such terror!" He swore a mighty oath to be revenged on the monster, and lost no time in summoning three-and-thirty of his men-at-arms.

"We must sail to Bamburgh," he told them. "We must land by Spindleston Hill and quell the loathsome creature."

He and his men set to and built a strong ship. Childwynde ordered the carpenters to make the masts from rowan wood. "I fear witchcraft is at work in Bamburgh," he warned. "Rowan wood will defeat any evil spell that is spun against us." And then without more delay they set off for Bamburgh, their sails of finest silk fluttering in a fair wind. They made a swift journey across the sea until they saw the castle towering above the rocky shore.

Now it happened that the Queen looked down from her tower and caught sight of sunlight glancing off the silken sails of a gallant ship. She knew at once who it was and why he came. Quickly she called up her demon servants to sink Childwynde's ship before it could land. But her spells were powerless against the magic of the rowan wood. So then in her fury she ordered the dreaded Laidley Worm to stop the ship.

The worm uncurled itself from the hill and crawled down to the shore. It burrowed under the sand until it was beneath the keel of Childwynde's ship and then it reared up. The ship rocked and began to heel over.

"Man the main brace!" shouted Childwynde. "Put about before we sink!"

The crew steered frantically for the shore with the monster's terrible breath behind them. As soon as they reached shallow water, Childwynde leapt from the ship and waded to dry land. He had only a moment to draw his sword before the worm was upon him.

To his amazement, the monster did not attack him. Instead, it hung its great head as a tear rolled from its bloodshot eye.

"Put down your sword. I will not harm you." Its voice was as soft as a summer wind. "I have been bewitched. If you will kiss me three times you will break the spell."

Chapter Five

A Happy Ending

Childwynde hesitated. Was this another trick? Were they false tears? Should he kiss the beast or kill the beast?

The monster spoke again. "Put down your sword, I beg you. Kiss me before the sun sets, before it is too late to save me." There was something about the monster's mournful, pleading look that melted Childwynde's heart. He shuddered as he bent forward to kiss its slimy, scaly face.

At the third kiss, the worm gave a shrieking hiss as its great body began to change. Slowly its coils sank into the sand, and in their place a figure rose up like a flower opening. It was Margaret. She shivered in the cold wind and Childwynde wrapped his cloak round her. She was the most beautiful maiden he had ever seen. "We must hurry," she whispered and pointed towards the castle. "My wicked stepmother bewitched me. She has magic powers and she means to do more evil."

Childwynde took her hand and together they ran across the shore, up the stone steps that led to the castle and through its great doors. The Queen met them on the stair, pale and afraid, twisting her wicked hands. She knew that her power was leaving her. There was no spell she could spin to avoid her fate.

Childwynde stood before her holding a twig of rowan. "Woe to you, you wicked woman!" he cried. "You deserve a horrible death for the suffering you have caused. As you bewitched Margaret, so shall you be bewitched. You shall become a loathsome toad, crawling in the mud for all your days. You shall never be saved!"

And with that, Childwynde touched the witch queen with the rowan twig. Her body began to shrink and shrivel until she was changed into an enormous scaly toad. It crawled clumsily down the castle stairs and disappeared behind a rock.

The King was overjoyed to find his beloved daughter alive again, and thanked Childwynde for saving them both from the witch's wicked wiles. Amid great rejoicing, Margaret and her lord were married and – of course – lived happily ever after.

As for the toad, people say that it is still seen to this day, lurking under the castle walls at Bamburgh. They say that every seven years it creeps out at night in search of innocent maidens.

Stories from a
variety of cultures

A Long Way Home

Chapter One

I was suffocating. The midday sun beat down on my head, and my pet mongoose, Nikki, was curled round my neck. I was desperate to get away quickly, but there was something I had to do first. With a quick glance over my shoulder, I knelt down by the cobra's bamboo cage, still breathing hard from my running. The cobra was coiled, sleeping innocently, as I lifted out its cold, firm body. It slithered away towards the old deserted mosque.

My plan to steal the snake for ransom had gone horribly wrong. Its owner, the snake charmer, had spotted me and was now out to get me. So was his friend, an even more scary person known as "the pickpocket man". It was rumoured that he kidnapped children, taught them to become pickpockets and turned them into his slaves.

I ran on, dodging in and out of the lanes of our slum colony. Only when Nikki and I had reached the main road did I breathe freely. At last the slum colony was behind me.

Endless streams of traffic choked the road. Cycles, cars, motorbikes, rickshaws, bullock and horse carts, buses, lorries and even a camel! Above the hubbub I heard a shout: "Look, isn't that Rashid? There, on the other side of the road. Quick! Get him before he runs away!"

I called to one of the dozens of cyclists pedalling by, "Hey mister, give us a ride to the bus station!" Ignoring his "Get lost kid!" I hopped side saddle onto his carrier, then bounded off as he cycled past the bus station a short distance on.

"Thanks!" I shouted. The bus station was like a giant anthill, teeming with people coming and going. The noise and fumes were overwhelming.

I located the bus to my aunt's village, dug into my pocket and presented ten rupees. It was all my sister Shama's savings. The conductor scowled.

"You trying to be funny? It's fifty rupees. Go on, vanish!"

Now what was I to do? If I wasn't nabbed by one of the men chasing me, my father was bound to punish me. A voice in my head piped up, "You could always pick someone's pocket." No! I'd got into enough trouble today. My only way out was to find work, save up a day's wage to buy my ticket, and go to Aunty Kulsum until things had quietened down. The question was, what should I go for? A roadside café? Or would a luggage porter in the bus station be better?

CHOICE 1 Porter in the bus station (Go to page 38.)

CHOICE 2 Tea boy in a café (Go to page 39.)

Choice 1

Porter in the bus station

"Sir, sir, let me carry your suitcase."

"Excuse me, madam, that looks heavy. Here, give it to me…"

"Show me your identity card first. There are too many thieves around."

"I haven't got an I.D., but you can trust me."

"Huh!"

A policeman swaggered up, swinging his cane. Nikki poked his head out of my shirtfront. I pushed him down.

"This boy says he is a porter, but can't show me an I.D.!"

The policeman stuck out his stomach and flexed his cane.

"Where are you from? Who gave you permission to hang about here? Turn out your pockets! Ah!" He snatched Shama's ten-rupee note. "A pickpocket, huh? Come to the police station and I'll charge you!"

"Sir, my sister gave me that note."

He grabbed my collar and tried to drag me with him. I struggled – there was a tearing sound, but I broke free and ran.

Choice 2

Tea boy in a café

A long row of shabby cafés lined the street next to the bus station. Huge pots of food simmered on stoves. I tried the Happy Diner Café.

I whispered, "Nikki, you stay hidden, otherwise we don't eat today!"

To my joy, the owner said, "Yes, you can start now, but one mistake and you're out. There are plenty of boys looking for work."

He threw me a greyish tea cloth and passed over a plate of rice and dahl and pickle. "Table three."

For the next hour I was kept busy rushing about with plates of food. I managed to feed Nikki with the leftovers. People came and went but no one left me a tip. It was dark and I was starving and feeling weak.

"Table seven." My boss handed me a plate. As I hurried over to the customer, a skinny cat suddenly streaked from under a chair. I tripped and the plate of steaming food went flying – all over a policeman who had just walked into the café. His face was purple with rage.

I fled.

Chapter Two

"You looking for somewhere to sleep tonight?"

A boy of my age and size appeared from nowhere.

"I saw what happened. Come on, there's a whole gang of us living near the tracks at the railway station. I'm Munna. What's your name?"

I told him and introduced Nikki.

"What do you do?"

"Nothing really – I've run away from home…"

"So have most of us. Some of us don't have families. Some of us have fathers who beat us – that's why we're on our own. But it's fun here, you'll see." He flashed me a smile. I liked him immediately.

"I shine shoes and carry loads for passengers. Other boys work in cafés and sell cups of tea to travellers. Just don't get mixed up with the pickpockets' gang," he warned. "They'll get you into trouble."

What could I do? Of course! There were lots of things I was good at – card tricks, telling fortunes (or pretending to!) and I was a contortionist. Father had taught me to twist myself into bendy shapes. I could lie on my tummy and bring my heels over my head. I could walk on my hands. I could make Nikki jump through a ring. Suddenly I felt quite cheerful. In no time at all I would have collected enough money to buy a bus ticket to my aunt's village.

Munna led me to a group of boys who were all squatting on the ground and eating from a large steel plate.

"He doesn't have anywhere to go," he explained.

The oldest-looking boy smiled warmly. "Come on, kid. Here, help yourself."

For the first time in twenty-four hours, I felt I was among friends. We slept on pieces of sacking behind some bushes alongside the tracks, and I felt quite safe with all the other boys.

Next morning, Munna took me to a standpipe where we both washed and scrubbed our teeth with neem twigs, and competed to see who could spit the furthest. The gang had brewed some tea on a wood fire, and we had that and biscuits for breakfast. Only one or two had a change of clothes.

The rest slept, worked and played in the same ragged shorts and shirts, night and day.

Soon, Munna went off cheerfully with his shoeshine kit, Ramesh went off to his café job and the others also disappeared. I was left by myself with Nikki. How should I make some money?

CHOICE 1 Card tricks and fortune telling (Go to page 43.)

CHOICE 2 Gymnastics and stunts with Nikki (Go to page 44.)

Choice 1

Card tricks and fortune telling

I set up my little magic centre on a flattened
cardboard box next to a popcorn seller on
Platform 5.

"Roll up, roll up! Come and see my card tricks!
Come and find out if it's your lucky day. Will you win
the lottery? Will your wife have a baby boy?"

Hundreds of travellers went past. Muslim
women in black burkhas, Hindu priests from South
India, tall Sikhs with brightly coloured turbans, soldiers going
home on leave…

A bored-looking soldier came up. "Show us your tricks."

I shuffled my pack of cards and invited him to pick one.

"Aha! You have picked the ace of hearts." The man's mouth
fell open.

"And that means you will be lucky in love. This is the year
your parents will choose a beautiful bride for you…"

Suddenly there was a roar. It was the policeman from
yesterday.

"I know you! Come along, you don't have a licence."

I took to my heels, leaving behind the sound of the popcorn
seller's laughter.

Choice 2

Gymnastics and stunts with Nikki

I flung a flattened cardboard box on the platform, near the water cooler, and spat on my hands.

"Roll up, roll up! Come and see the champion Olympic gymnast! Chosen already for the 2012 Olympics. Only 50 paise to admire my feats. Roll up, roll up!"

I limbered up by touching my toes, stretching up, then, going down on my tummy, I brought my feet over my head and held my heels. A few people had gathered to watch. I turned a few cartwheels and walked on my hands.

"Isn't he clever, Papa?" I heard a girl say admiringly.

As I walked backwards, someone tickled my feet with a feather. I fell flat on my face and a roar of laughter went up.

"Hey, you rascal. What are you playing at?" It was the policeman from yesterday, standing over me. "Explain yourself!"

Chapter Three

All my efforts at making money ended in nothing but disappointment. I wished I were like that cobra – curled up in a bamboo cage, letting life pass me by. As far as I knew, no one was missing me. My father was probably relieved that I had disappeared. My mother was too tired to care. Only Shama would be thinking about me, and there was no way I could contact her. We didn't have a phone and I didn't even have enough money to buy a postcard to send her.

Little did she know that all this was because of her. I had tried to kidnap the cobra to make some money for her schoolbooks. We have no spare cash at home for things like that. Me, I play truant all the time. But Shama's really clever.

That night, I sat with the boys and we ate together in a circle as usual. The glow from the fire illuminated their faces, lending them an angelic softness. No bullies here, I thought. We had all suffered too much. Did the others have hopes for a better future, a better life? And yet, everything we needed to live was right there – a meal, companionship, a fire and somewhere to sleep.

"You could make money travelling on the trains," one of the boys told me helpfully. "Run errands for passengers, look after babies while their mothers go for a wash, fetch cups of tea at stops. And people share their picnic meals. Lovely home-cooked food. Yum, yum." He rubbed his tummy.

The stars hung low like glow-worms. Their winking seemed to beckon me to a new adventure. I dreamed of trains, their mournful, owl-like whistles calling, "Come away, come away."

My mind was made up. But which direction should I travel? North or south? Shimla or Chennai?

"Where shall we go Nikki?"

CHOICE 1 The train to Shimla (Go to page 47.)

CHOICE 2 The train to Chennai (Go to page 48.)

Choice 1

The train to Shimla

"Sit still!" The woman with four kids pulled two of them from the window, where they were hanging out. The toddler began wailing and the baby started to whimper like a hungry kitten. "Here, hold her for a minute." She thrust the bundle into my arms and rummaged in one of her many bags. "Now be QUIET!" she instructed the toddler, handing him a biscuit.

"Me too, me too!" yelled the infants, like twin parrots, turning round from the window.

"Dear God, is this going to continue all the way to Shimla?" grumbled an old man, crackling his newspaper.

"Don't worry, I'll look after the children," I said.

"Thank you. If you could take care of them, I might get some sleep. We're going to meet my husband – he's a soldier and he's never even seen the baby," she explained.

She fell asleep instantly, like a light being switched off. Then, I heard the ominous words, "Tickets please!"

I thrust the baby at the sleepy mother. "I have to go," I whispered, and I squeezed my way into the corridor.

Choice 2

The train to Chennai

"Here boy, at the next stop get me four teas, plenty of sugar. I'll give you a rupee."

"Make that two," I said, casually.

"All right, two."

Chennai was more than twenty-four hours away, almost at the toe of India. Maybe I could save up and buy a supply of sweets to sell on the train. There were plenty of parents who would want to keep their kids quiet. Maybe I could fetch drinking water for passengers, or lift down their luggage, or dispose of their leftovers and wrappings. Why hadn't the railways thought of these useful services?

Suddenly, I was forced back to Earth, as I heard the words, "Tickets please!"

Chapter Four

The train was trundling through grimy slums and makeshift colonies, just like the one I came from. We had left the great bustling station at Delhi behind but hadn't picked up speed.

I had to get out of the moving train, but how? I realised I was terrified of being caught. I was scared of so many strangers. And I was frightened of going a thousand miles away from my home.

The squeal of brakes gave me my chance. The train stopped, I wrenched open the door, looked right and left, and jumped onto the track. We couldn't be more than 20 miles or so from Delhi, and it would still be possible to return to my friends in the station. The train had stopped next to a large village on the outskirts of the capital. But how was I going to get back?

In front of me, a tractor was trundling down the road to Delhi, pulling a trailer with a load of hay. Tied up in the shade of a tree was a camel with a cart behind it. The cart was full of sacks of vegetables. The camel driver was stretched out in the shade listening to songs on his radio.

CHOICE 1 The tractor (Go to page 50.)

CHOICE 2 The camel cart (Go to page 51.)

Choice 1

The tractor

The hay made me want to sneeze. It scratched my legs and tickled my nose. I burrowed under it and tried to enjoy the ride. At one point, the driver of the tractor stopped at a wayside café for a cup of tea. My tongue was hanging out of my mouth, I was so parched. It was afternoon and I hadn't eaten or drunk all day. I wished that I could sneak out and find a drink.

After what seemed like hours, we arrived back in the city as the sun was going down. I peeked out of my covering of straw and recognised some landmarks. I would be able to walk to the railway station from there.

Choice 2

The camel cart

The journey back to Delhi took hours and hours. Camels are not built like racehorses – it was plod-plod-plod all the way. The camel driver played his radio very loudly and when he came to a police checkpoint they made him show his licence, so I burrowed under a sack of potatoes. It was hard to breathe and I could feel a dozen sneezes, ready to give me away, but we were waved through.

Then the cart halted and I heard him talking to himself. "What was that noise?" he said.

My heart stopped. I had been singing along to the song on the radio, which was a favourite of Shama's. I lay still under the sacks and to my great relief he said "Hup!" to the camel and we were on our way again.

At a junction near the railway station I crawled out and hopped off. I felt a big sneeze coming, but it didn't matter any more. I would soon be with my friends again.

Chapter Five

To get to the camp, I had to cross a bridge. I saw the glow of firelight in the distance.

Then, to my horror, I noticed a policeman on the platform just below – the policeman I had begun to know too well. Nikki, sensing my alarm, stuck his sharp nose out of my shirt and sniffled. I retraced my steps, thinking it would be wiser to wait until he had left.

But whom should I see but another familiar figure – the pickpocket man!

Where should I go? Both ways were full of danger.

CHOICE 1 Dodge the policeman to get to the boys' campfire (Go to page 53.)

CHOICE 2 Turn back and dodge past the pickpocket man (Go to page 54.)

Choice 1

Dodge the policeman to get to the boys' campfire

With all my senses alert, I climbed slowly down the platform stairs. The policeman was standing next to the last step, looking bored. I tiptoed by, then broke into a run, but didn't notice the popcorn seller bending over to tie up his goods. I collided with him violently and all his popcorn spilled onto the ground. "Oi! What're you doing?" yelled the policeman. "Stop!"

I kept running, leaping over every obstacle, until I came to the fire.

(Go to page 55.)

Choice 2

Turn back and dodge past the pickpocket man

I hid behind a large woman who was carrying a heavy bag in each hand. She was scolding her small, skinny husband as he pulled along an enormous suitcase. I knew that soon we were going to pass the pickpocket man, but hoped that the woman's bulk would hide me. Unfortunately, she stubbed her toe on a piece of paving. "Ow!" she exclaimed, stopping so abruptly that I tripped on her heel. She lost her balance and fell heavily.

I didn't pause, but turned round and raced back the way I had come.

(Go to page 55.)

Chapter Five *continued*

Although it was late, all the lads were round the fire, their faces aglow.

"Rashid! You're back! We were so worried! Look, there's a little food left over." Everyone was talking at the same time, and only then did I notice the stranger with them – a young woman dressed in a yellow shalwar kameez.

"Meet Veena, Rashid," said Munna. "She's our social worker and she's been looking for you everywhere."

But another girl was squatting next to her. A girl who came flying to throw her arms around me. "Rashid! You're safe! Where have you been? Come home – no one will punish you. Veena has been talking to Father and Mother. Everything will be all right."

The policeman had also arrived, puffing loudly. "Come here, you rascal! This time I won't let you go." Veena showed him her I.D. "It's all right, brother," she said respectfully. "I will take care of him." He moved off grumpily.

The pickpocket man had also appeared. He stood a little apart, shaking his fist and muttering to himself. "Hey, Grandad!" Munna called to the pickpocket man. "No use coming here. You're trespassing! Go away or we'll call the police!" Everyone roared with laughter.

"We were lucky that we traced you after you were reported missing," said Veena. "Don't worry, all is forgiven. And you have a choice – to go home to your family, or to come with some of the boys who've agreed to join our children's home. You'll get proper schooling and learn different skills – building, tailoring, bike repairs, welding, all sorts of trades. One day you could support your family."

Then I looked at my sister's pleading expression. There were tears in her eyes. I had missed her and the little ones very much, but I was afraid of what would happen once I got home. It wouldn't be easy, but I couldn't abandon her or my mother.

I couldn't decide.

"If you go home," warned Veena, "there must be no more thieving. You could still come to the day centre and learn some skills." My heart sank. How could I face my father again? Would the snake charmer still be after me? What should I do?